LEK

the Elephant Whisperer

Based on a
True Story

By Sylvia M. Medina

Illustrations by Andreas Wessel-Therhorn

green kids club

Noah Text®

Noah Text®

The **Noah Text®** Chapter Books have been carefully selected and curated to meet the needs of all readers – and striving and struggling readers in particular – by providing superior text accessibility. Noah Text® books are rendered in **Noah Text®, a patented evidence-based methodology for displaying text that increases reading skill.**

Grounded in the science of reading, Noah Text® is a specialized scaffolded text that shows **syllable patterns** within words by highlighting them with bold and unbold and marking **long vowels** (vowels that "say their own names"). Here are some examples:

entertainment	⇨	**en**ter**tain**ment
beautiful	⇨	**beau**tiful
photosynthesis	⇨	**pho**to**syn**the**sis**
comprehension	⇨	**com**pre**hen**sion
ironic	⇨	i**ron**ic
lieutenant	⇨	**lieu**ten**ant**
achievement	⇨	a**chieve**ment
epitome	⇨	e**pit**ome
ideology	⇨	i**de**ol**ogy**
coordination	⇨	**co**or**di**na**tion**

By showing readers the structure of words, Noah Text® enhances reading skills, freeing up cognitive resources that readers can devote to comprehension. Noah Text® simulates simpler writing systems (e.g., Finland's) in which learning to read is easier due to visible, predictable word patterns. As a result, Noah Text® increases reading fluency, stamina, accuracy, and confidence while building skills that transfer to plain text reading.

Highly recommended by structured literacy specialists, Noah Text® is effective for developing, struggling, and dyslexic readers and for multilingual learners. Noah Text® enables resistant and struggling readers to advance their reading skills beyond basic proficiency so that they can tackle higher-level learning.

Readers find Noah Text® intuitive and easy to use, requiring little to no instruction to get started. A sound key that further explains how Noah Text® works can be found at the back of this book.

For further information on Noah Text® and its products, please visit www.noahtext.com.

Dear Parents, Educators, and Striving English-Language Readers,

As individuals develop the ability to read beyond the elementary level, their challenge is to build on a basic awareness of how patterns of letters stand for sounds and how those sounds come together to make words. Readers who learn the letter patterns in one-syllable words are poised to recognize them in longer, multisyllable words.

For struggling readers, however, long words can appear to be a sea of individual letters whose syllable sub-divisions are hard to discern. This series from Noah Text® highlights where syllable breaks occur, while also signaling long vowels -- those that "say their own names."   These visual cues help struggling readers decode words more easily and read more fluently and accurately.

Now, with Noah Text® Chapter Books, all individuals can learn to read with less effort, empowering them to experience enriching literature and enlightening informational texts.

Miriam Cherkes-Julkowski, Ph.D.
Professor, Educational Psychology (retired)
Educational Diagnostician and Consultant

About the Author -
Sylvia M. Medina
is the president, primary author, and creative lead of the Green Kids Club. She has spent her career focused on environmental issues and helping to preserve animal welfare. She hopes to teach children the importance of helping to save our world and its animals.

About the Illustrator -
Andreas Wessel-Therhorn
is from Münster, Germany. He has been working in animation for more than 32 years for, among others, Walt Disney Feature Animation, Warner Bros., and Universal Studios. His many credits include Hercules, Tarzan, Fantasia 2000, and Mary Poppins Returns.

Special thanks to our photographers -
Bruce Miller, Avijan Saha, and Biplap Hazra

Contributors -
Ry Emmerson, Charlotte Broussard,
Shelley Mascia, and Joy Eagle

green kids club
www.greenkidsclub.com

LEK

the **Elephant Whisperer**

Based on a True Story

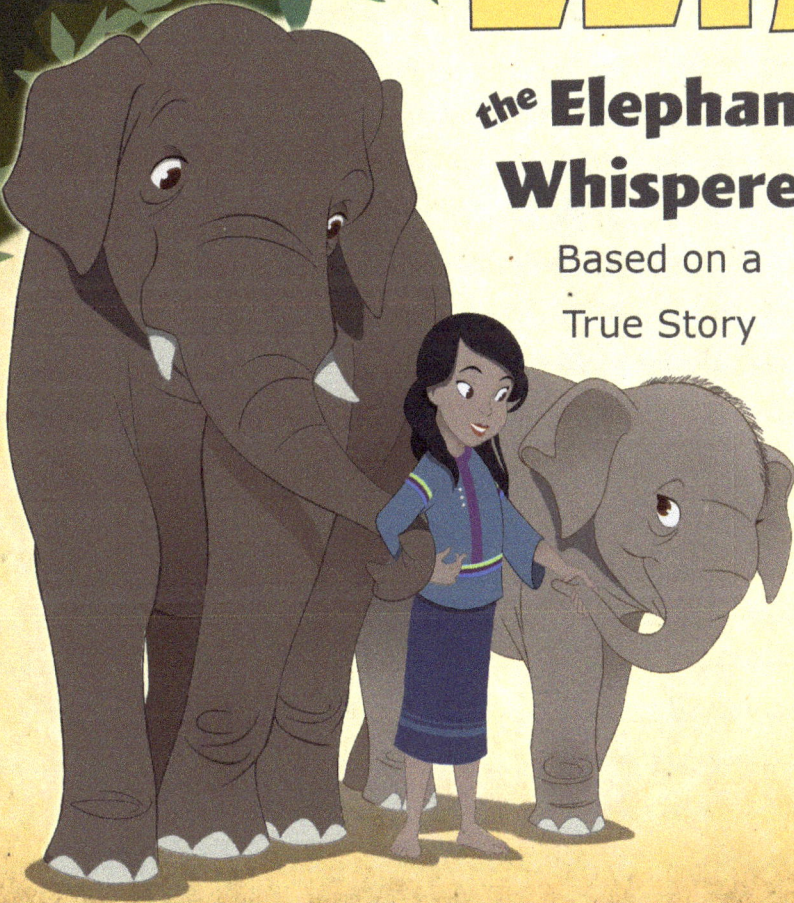

By Sylvia M. Medina

Illustrations by Andreas Wessel-Therhorn

green kids club

Noah Text

CONTENTS

Little Lek the Br**a**ve

Little Lek was **play**ing in the cr**ee**k.

Sh**e** lived in **Thai**land, a **beau**tiful **coun**try full of **animals** and birds.

As sh**e** pl**a**yed, sh**e** h**ea**rd the l**ea**ves **rus**tle in the wind, and a voice **whis**per, "D**o**n't move!"

The voice of the tr**ee**s m**a**de the **lit**tle girl stop **play**ing in the cr**ee**k. Sh**e** looked up and saw a **mas**sive t**i**ger **walk**ing str**ai**ght **to**wards her.

1

His t<u>ai</u>l was **flick**er**ing** back and forth as h<u>e</u> snarled at the child –

ggrrrrrrrrrrrrrrrrr.

Little Lek tr<u>ie</u>d not to move. Her heart **pound**ed in her chest, and her f<u>a</u>ce flushed as sh<u>e</u> st<u>a</u>red **in**tent**ly in**to its eyes. The **ti**ger stopped, and sh<u>e</u> could s<u>ee</u> her **re**flec**tion** in his d<u>ee</u>p **yel**l<u>o</u>w eyes. Sh<u>e</u> could s<u>ee</u> its long, sharp claws, h<u>u</u>ge fangs, and smell his **ac**rid breath. Sh<u>e</u> **trem**bled but tr<u>ie</u>d not to move.

M<u>o</u>tion**less**, the two of them st<u>a</u>red at <u>e</u>ach **oth**er.

Sudden**ly**, a large **Horn**bill swooped down from the tr<u>ee</u>s, **scr<u>ee</u>ch**ing, "Caw, caw, caw."

The **ti**ger looked up at the bird, **bre<u>a</u>k**ing the spell.

With one last glance at the **lit**tle girl, h<u>e</u> turned his head and walked back **in**to the d<u>ee</u>p **re**cess of the **for**est **jun**gle.

Sh<u>e</u> stood there for a **mo**ment, **st<u>a</u>r**ing at where the **ti**ger had been, and **sl<u>ow</u>**ly s<u>i</u>ghed in **re**li<u>e</u>f.

Then sh**e** looked **a**round, **search**ing for the **ti**ger. Not **see**ing him, sh**e** tore out of the **jun**gle as fast as her **lit**tle legs could **ca**rry her.

Sh**e** ran **fast**er than sh**e** had **ev**er run **be**fore. **Huff**ing and **puff**ing, sh**e** ran **un**til sh**e** r**e**ached her **fam**ily's hut.

Little Lek cr**i**ed out, "**Grand**father, **Grand**father, help m**e**." **Grand**father and **Moth**er c**a**me **rush**ing out of the hut and saw Lek's t**e**ar-st**ai**ned f**a**ce.

Grandfather ran **to**wards her and knelt **be**side her, "Lek, what's wrong?"

She sat down on the ground and **start**ed **sob**bing. "**Grand**father, I saw the **big**gest **ti**ger, and I think he **want**ed to eat me. But I heard the trees **tell**ing me not to move, so I stood as still as I could, and then he walked away."

The old man wiped the tears from the **lit**tle girl's face. "Lek, I knew you could do this."

Lek looked at her **grand**father, tears still **stream**ing from her eyes. "**Grand**father, I was so scared. But I did what the trees told me."

Grandfather said, "You're **ver**y brave, and now I know you're the one!"

"What do you mean, I'm the one?" she asked, still **trem**bling from her **en**coun**ter** with the **ti**ger.

"I have **cho**sen you to lead the **peo**ple in **pro**tect**ing** our **animals** and their homes," the old **Sha**man said, **spread**ing his arms and hands as if to **em**brace the world. Her **moth**er reached out and held Lek in her arms.

Lek **nod**ded, looked up **in**to the trees, and saw the Great **Horn**bill **watch**ing her **in**tent**ly**. She had heard their voice.

Lek would **al**ways **re**mem**ber** the **ti**ger's deep, **penetrat**ing eyes. In fact, they would **re**mind her of the eyes of the **elephant** that changed her life **for**ev**er**.

Lek and Her **Grand**father

Lek's **Grand**father was a **Sha**man —
he **be**lieved in the **spir**its of the world and its
animals. He taught and helped the **peo**ple
from Lek's **vil**lage, but he **most**ly told them
about the **beau**ty of the earth and its
animals. The **vil**lag**ers** did not **al**ways **lis**ten,
but Lek took in **ever**y**thing** he told them.

Sometimes, she would walk with her
grandfather in the **jun**gle as he showed her
little bugs, trees, **elephants**, and birds. He
taught her the **im**por**tance** of **lov**ing **na**ture
and all its **animals** and to have **rev**er**ence** for
the earth and its **in**habitants.

One day, **af**ter they had spent a day in the **jun**gle, Lek was **sit**ting **qui**etly in her home, **play**ing. **Hear**ing a noise, she looked up and saw her **grand**father **com**ing **to**wards their hut. **Quick**ly, she sat down and pulled a **blank**et over her.

"Where's the **ba**by **mon**key?" asked **Grand**father **Sha**man as he **en**tered Lek's house.

Lek was **sit**ting on the couch with a blue **blan**ket with **flow**ers on her lap.

She held it **close**ly. "What **ba**by **mon**key?" she asked **in**no**cent**ly.

Suddenly, the **blan**ket **rust**led, and a **lit**tle head popped out.

"I knew you had her," laughed **Grand**father **Sha**man. "It's time to take her back to her **jun**gle home."

"**Grand**father, I don't want to. I love her and want her to stay with me **for**ever," she said **stub**born**ly**, **jut**ting her chin out in **de**fiance.

"Lek, I've told you not to get **at**tached to the **an**imals we bring home. I don't want you **nam**ing them or **treat**ing them like your **ba**by. They're wild, and **af**ter we have helped them, we need to **re**turn them to their **families**," he said, **sit**ting **be**side her.

"Let's take her home," he said as he scooped up the **mon**key.

Taking Lek by the hand, the two hiked through the deep green lush **jun**gle **un**til they found a **clear**ing with large trees and a troop of **mon**keys **play**ing **o**ver**head** in its **branch**es.

Grandfather knelt and looked **in**to Lek's eyes, "Child, are you **read**y to give the **lit**tle **mon**key to her **family**?"

Lek's eyes were **brim**ming with tears as she **nod**ded. "**Good**bye, my **ba**by," she **whis**pered, **hug**ging her **tight**ly.

The **ba**by **mon**key hugged her back and then **scur**ried off **in**to the trees while they looked on.

"This is where she **be**longs. You have done a great thing **to**day," her **grand**father said **sol**emn**ly**.

Through her **stream**ing tears, Lek looked at her **grand**father and **nod**ded.

Grandfather **Sha**man said, "Let's **go**, Lek. You have **prov**en that you can help **oth**er **animals** who need help. I can now trust you to help them."

Just then, she heard the **rus**tling of the trees in the wind. **Look**ing up, she thought she saw the trees nod in **agree**ment. In the **dis**tance, she heard the **caw**ing of the Great **Horn**bill.

Going to School

Lek sat on the ground, **watch**ing as the boys tromped down the road to school.

One of the boys **eye**balled the **lit**tle girl and said, "What are you **look**ing at, girl? What do you want?"

Lek shrugged, "I want to go to school."

The boy laughed, "Girls don't go to school. **On**ly us boys! Where did you get such a **sil**ly idea?"

The boys **start**ed **laugh**ing.

Lek got up and ran off to her home with the boys' **laugh**ter still **ring**ing in her ears.

"**Mom**ma," she huffed as she **en**tered the hut, "I want to go to school!"

Her **moth**er looked at her and said, "Lek, yo**u** will **nev**er g**o** to school. School is **on**ly for boys."

Lek **be**gan **weep**ing. Her **moth**er looked at her **sor**r**o**w**ful**ly, then stood up and **de**cl**a**red, "Lek, yo**u**'re r**i**ght—yo**u** will g**o** to school."

"**Re**ally, **Mom**ma?" sh**e** asked.

"Trust m**e**, my **daugh**ter," sh**e** **re**pl**i**ed.

The next d**a**y, Lek's **moth**er c**a**me to her. "Lek, **I** have **de**c**i**ded that **I** am **go**ing to send yo**u** to school. **I** d**o**n't c**a**re that yo**u**'re a girl. **Grand**f**a**ther would have **want**ed yo**u** to g**o**. If yo**u** get an **ed**u**ca**tion, **may**b**e** one d**a**y yo**u** can l**ea**d our **coun**try in **pro**tect**ing** w**i**ld **an**imals and their h**o**mes. But yo**u** must kn**o**w that this will b**e** a long, hard **jour**n**e**y." Then sh**e** **hes**it**a**ted, looked at her, and said, they w**o**n't **wel**come yo**u**."

Ignor**ing** this last **com**ment, Lek hugged her. "**Moth**er, Thank yo̲u̲! I̲ can't **be**li̲e̲ve it!!!"

Getting an **ed**u̲c̲a̲tion was not **go**̲ing to be **eas**y, **be**̲cause their **family** had to l̲eave their h̲ome and get jobs cl̲ose to the school. So̲, their **fam**ily had to move to the h̲ome of a man who had work for them.

Every**one** in her **family** had a job – from the **young**est to the **o̲ld**est. Lek's job was to t̲ake c̲are of the **o̲wn**er's pigs. The man led her to the **ar̲e̲a** where the pigs were. She̲ p̲eered **in**to the pen and saw ten **lit**tle **ba̲**by pigs **sle̲e̲p**ing **con**tent**ly**.

Lek **en**tered the pen and **start**ed **pick**ing e̲ach of them up. "O̲h, you̲'re so̲ cu̲te," she̲ laughed as she̲ **lift**ed e̲ach **lit**tle pig **a**bove her head. Their **lit**tle legs **dan**gled as they scr̲e̲amed and oinked **un**contro̲lla**bly**.

"Yo**u**'re all s**o** **fun**ny and **smell**y. But **I** **al**rea**dy** love **e**ach of yo**u**," sh**e** said, **lift**ing and **kiss**ing **e**ach **ba**by pig on their **lit**tle, fat, pink, and **dirt**y snouts. The **lit**tle pigs **slow**ly stopped **strug**gling and let her pl**ay** with them.

Sh**e** laughed and **start**ed **nam**ing **e**ach one of them: "Your n**a**me is **Pudg**y, and your name is **Stink**y." Sh**e** **contin**u**ed** **un**til sh**e** got to the last small **ba**by runt: "And yo**u**'re my **Lit**tle **Ba**by," she b**e**amed, her eyes **shin**ing with **hap**pin**ess**.

In t**i**me, the **lit**tle pigs **be**c**a**me Lek's best friends. **S**he would h**o**ld her **ba**by pigs, who would squeal in **de**light when sh**e** pl**a**yed with them.

But her **hap**pin**ess** with the **ba**by pigs was short-lived, for sh**e** was **a**bout to g**o** to school.

On the first d<u>a</u>y of school, dressed in her **u**ni**form** and **ba**re**foot**, Lek walked **shy**ly **in**to the **class**room. There, sh<u>e</u> f<u>a</u>ced a **class**room of boys **star**ing **in**tent**ly** at her.

"What is sh<u>e</u> **do**ing h<u>e</u>re?" yelled one of the boys. The **teach**er looked up from her desk with her cold, **gla**r**ing** eyes.

The **teach**er said, "Girl – what do yo<u>u</u> want? D<u>o</u>n't yo<u>u</u> kn<u>o</u>w **on**ly boys can g<u>o</u> to school?"

Lek's **lit**tle chin **quiv**ered as sh<u>e</u> said **brave**ly, "<u>I</u> am h<u>e</u>re to g<u>o</u> to school."

The **teach**er got up from her desk and walked out the door **in**to the **hall**w<u>a</u>y, **yell**ing for the **prin**ci**pal**. Lek stood **si**lent**ly with**out **mov**ing. The boys sat in their ch<u>a</u>irs, **snick**er**ing** at her.

One of them said, "Look at that girl's h<u>a</u>ir – **does**n't sh<u>e</u> **ev**er wash it? Sh<u>e</u> looks l<u>i</u>ke a **smell**y fox."

The **teach**er walked back in. "Leave her alone. We have **school**work to do," she **re**tort**ed an**grily.

"Sit down, girl," she **mum**bled. "I can't **be**lieve I have to put up with this. Don't blame me if you don't like it here." The boys in the **class**room **be**gan **laugh**ing **loud**ly and **ma**king pig **nois**es, for they all knew Lek was **ta**king care of pigs.

"Oink, oink, oink, the pig girl is here," **crack**led one of the boys. The **oth**ers **start**ed **shout**ing–"Pig Girl – Pig Girl – Pig Girl." One of the **oth**er boys said, "No, she is the **Stink**y Fox Girl. That is what we will call her!"

The **teach**er laughed with the boys.

Lek stood **si**lently as the boys **be**rated her. She was not **go**ing to let them see the tears that were **well**ing up **in**side of her.

Every day, the boys at school **treat**ed Lek **cru**elly. **Some**times, they called her names, and **oth**er times, they pulled her hair and did **ter**rible things to her. Lek would just close her eyes and see **her**self **sit**ting with her **ba**by pigs. She **re**fused to cry. She would stand still with her head held high and her eyes closed **un**til they stopped. The **tea**cher **of**ten watched the boys through the school **win**dows but did not stop them from **taunt**ing her.

At the end of each day, Lek would run out the school door as fast as her **lit**tle legs would **ca**rry her **un**til she reached the pen. She would sit on the ground with her **lit**tle pigs as they crawled on her lap and in her arms. She would hold and kiss them, and they would **nuz**zle and kiss her back. With tears **stream**ing down her face, she would tell them of her **horri**ble day and then lie down in the pen with them while they all tried to **com**fort her.

These boys **tor**tured Lek **eve**ry day, but **de**spite it all, she worked to learn the **les**sons the **teach**er taught. The **teach**er's son was **es**pecially **cru**el to her.

One day, the boys hurt her **terribly**. Lek ran out of the **class**room to her **ba**by pigs, who by then had grown quite large. As she neared the pen, she called out their names, "**Lit**tle **Ba**by, **Stinky**! Where are you?"

Usually, the pigs would start **squeal**ing for joy as she ran up to them. But this day, **noth**ing but **si**lence **greet**ed her.

Lek ran **in**to the pen and did not see **an**y of her **ba**bies. She ran **in**to the yard, **yell**ing, "Where are my **ba**by pigs?"

Lek's **moth**er came out of the house and said, "Lek, they took them."

35

Lek **start**ed **run**ning **to**wards the road, where she saw a truck. She saw her pigs **be**ing **load**ed **on**to the truck one at a time. The pigs were **squeal**ing and **cry**ing. Then they saw her and stopped **squeal**ing. The man said, "What are you **do**ing here, girl?"

She said, "Those are my pigs. You can't take them."

"The **own**er sold them to me," he said. "We're **tak**ing them now. But they're so loud. Can you calm them down, please?"

"**O**kay, but please don't hurt them," Lek said.

Looking at her with his **bead**y **lit**tle black eyes, he said, "**O**kay."

Lek looked at her pigs – they calmed down when they saw her.

Lek then **re**al**ized** what had **hap**pened. She had raised the pigs so they could be **tak**en **a**way as food for **some**one to eat. She **start**ed **sob**bing **un**cont**ro**lla**bly** as the truck pulled **a**way.

With tears **blind**ing her eyes, she **be**gan **scream**ing and **yell**ing, "Don't take my **ba**bies, please, please."

She chased the truck **un**til she could no **long**er keep up with it. Lek **col**lapsed on the ground in a heap, **wail**ing and **cry**ing **un**cont**ro**lla**bly** .

Her **moth**er ran out and took her by the hand. **Moth**er took her **gin**ger**ly** and hugged her. She **nev**er saw her pigs **a**gain.

The next day, Lek went back to school. When **re**cess **be**gan, the **teach**er's son **start**ed **taunt**ing her, "Fox Girl, Fox Girl – where are your pigs now?" he laughed evilly.

A wave of **an**ger welled deep **in**side Lek. **Sud**den**ly** she ran at him, and **be**fore she could do **anything**, the **teach**er stopped her, **yell**ing **an**grily, "You go home – you're **nev**er to come back to this school **a**gain, Fox Girl!"

With her face flushed in **an**ger, Lek said, "I won't **ev**er come back to this school, **nev**er, **ev**er! But one day you'll see – you will see me **a**gain, and you will **sa**lute me," she yelled and ran off.

From then on, Lek vowed **nev**er to eat meat **a**gain, **es**pe**cial**ly pigs. She left this school and **at**tend**ed** a **Chris**tian school, where they **treat**ed her with **re**spect.

41

The **El**ephant Who Ch<u>a</u>nged Lek's L<u>i</u>fe

As Lek grew **<u>ol</u>d**er, sh<u>e</u> **re**mem**bered** **h<u>ea</u>r**ing **Grand**father **Sha**man's w<u>i</u>se words and the **wis**dom of her **moth**er. Sh<u>e</u> **com**pl<u>e</u>t**ed** her **school**ing wh<u>i</u>le **al**w<u>a</u>ys **try**ing to help as **man**y **an**i**mals** as **pos**si**ble**.

One d<u>ay</u>, Lek had left school with one of the **mis**sion<u>a</u>ri<u>e</u>s and heard a loud sound that **sound**ed l<u>i</u>ke an **el**ephant in **dis**tress. Lek said, "What is **hap**pen**ing**? Can w<u>e</u> g<u>o</u>, and s<u>ee</u>?"

B<u>e</u>fore the **mis**sion<u>a</u>**ry** could stop her, Lek had dashed **a**cross the r<u>oa</u>d to **in**ves**ti**g<u>a</u>te.

Before her was a bull **elephant** in chains, **try**ing to pull a **wood**en sled full of logs. Thr**ee** **ma**houts were all **a**round the **el**ephant as it **re**fused to move. One of the **ma**houts had a sharp **met**al hook on a rod, **hit**ting the **elephant** on the back of its head, wh**i**le **an**oth**er** hit it from the s**i**de, and **an**oth**er** from the back. The **elephant** was **scre**aming in p**ai**n. When Lek c**a**me **up**on the **elephant**, it looked at her with w**i**ld eyes and **con**tin**ued** to scr**ee**am.

Lek yelled, "Stop this – stop **hurt**ing him!"

The **mis**sion**ary** pulled her **a**s**i**de, "Lek, w**e** must l**ea**ve – yo**u** can't do this."

"But why won't they stop?" she asked **mis**erably.

"It's the **elephant**'s job – he's **re**fu**sing** to move – and they are **try**ing to make him work," he said.

"No – they have to stop," she wailed.

The sound of her voice made the **elephant** turn its head and look at Lek with the **deep**est, most **sorrowful** eyes she had ever seen. In its eyes, she saw a **fier**y red **re**flec**tion** of the men **beat**ing and **hurt**ing it.

"We must leave now. There's **noth**ing we can do!" said the **mis**sion**a**ry, **pull**ing Lek away from the **el**ephant.

Lek went home, and all she could hear and see that night was the **elephant scream**ing with its **penetrat**ing eyes. Lek's **jour**ney to save the **A**sian **Elephant** from the **cru**el**ty** of **cap**tivity by **hu**mans had **be**gun.

Saving Elephants

Lek **be**gan **Jum**bo **Ex**press, a group that would help save **elephants** from the **cru**elties of man. She would do **what**ever she could to get **peo**ple to help her. And she would **en**courage the **peo**ple who were **en**slaving the **elephants** to **re**lease them. But they **gen**erally **ig**nored her and just said, "There's **cra**zy Lek here **both**ering us **a**gain. She **does**n't know what she's **do**ing."

Lek would **ig**nore them, and she would try to **con**vince them to stop **en**slaving **elephants**. But **gen**erally, **noth**ing would work. **Dur**ing this time, she met an **in**credible **vet**erinarian, who would help her **when**ever she **need**ed him.

When Lek **trav**eled, she **start**ed **bring**ing **medicine** with her to treat **any** **elephants** that were **wound**ed. She did **what**ever she could to help care for them. **Event**u**ally**, she even found the **elephant** she had seen in the **for**est with its deep **penetrat**ing eyes and cleaned his wounds.

One day, as she went from **area** to **area**, she ran **in**to a man with deep cuts on his hands **result**ing from the **hor**rors of **elephant poach**ing. His hands looked **in**fect**ed**. He asked Lek to treat his wounds.

She laughed, "Why would I help **some**one like you who hurts **elephants**?"

"Oh, you're that **cra**zy **la**dy that **every**one says I should stay away from," he said. "I'm not **a**fraid of you – but my hands hurt so bad. Can you please help me?"

She said, "Even if you hurt the **elephants** – I will still help you."

H**e** watched her **qui**etly as sh**e** worked on his cuts.

As the d**a**ys went by, Lek **be**gan **help**ing all the **peo**ple of the **vil**lage with her **med**ic**a**tions. Soon, the **peo**ple who **o**wned the **cap**tive **elephants** c**a**me to **vis**it her. Lek sh**a**red her love of the **elephants** with them. **E**ven t**u**ally, sh**e** found that some of them were **be**gin**ning** to r**e**l**e**ase the **elephants** back **in**to the w**i**ld. Lek had **be**come one of them—and they were **start**ing to **lis**ten to her.

One d**a**y, Lek was called by one of the **vil**lag**ers be**cause a **moth**er **elephant** had just d**i**ed, and its **ba**by was **sit**ting there by the s**i**de of the tr**ee** where the **moth**er's **bod**y was still ch**a**ined. Next to the **ba**by was its **o**ld**er sis**ter. **Vis**u**a**lly **up**set, the two were **look**ing at their **moth**er. They had **no**where to g**o**.

The **ow**ners of the **elephants** asked Lek if sh<u>e</u> would t<u>a</u>ke the **ba**by and her **sis**ter. Sh<u>e</u> was s<u>o</u> **ex**c<u>it</u>ed that sh<u>e</u> brought them h<u>o</u>me and put them in her **back**yard. Sh<u>e</u> **be**gan to r<u>ai</u>se and c<u>a</u>re for the **lit**tle **el**ephants as sh<u>e</u> had learned from her **vil**lage friends.

These two **el**ephants grew to love Lek. Sh<u>e</u> c<u>a</u>red for them, took them for **el**ephant walks, slept with them, and m<u>a</u>de their milk. They thought of Lek as their **moth**er. Sh<u>e</u> could not b<u>e</u> far **a**w<u>a</u>y from them, or they would start **run**ning round and round with their <u>e</u>ars **fly**ing, **look**ing for her.

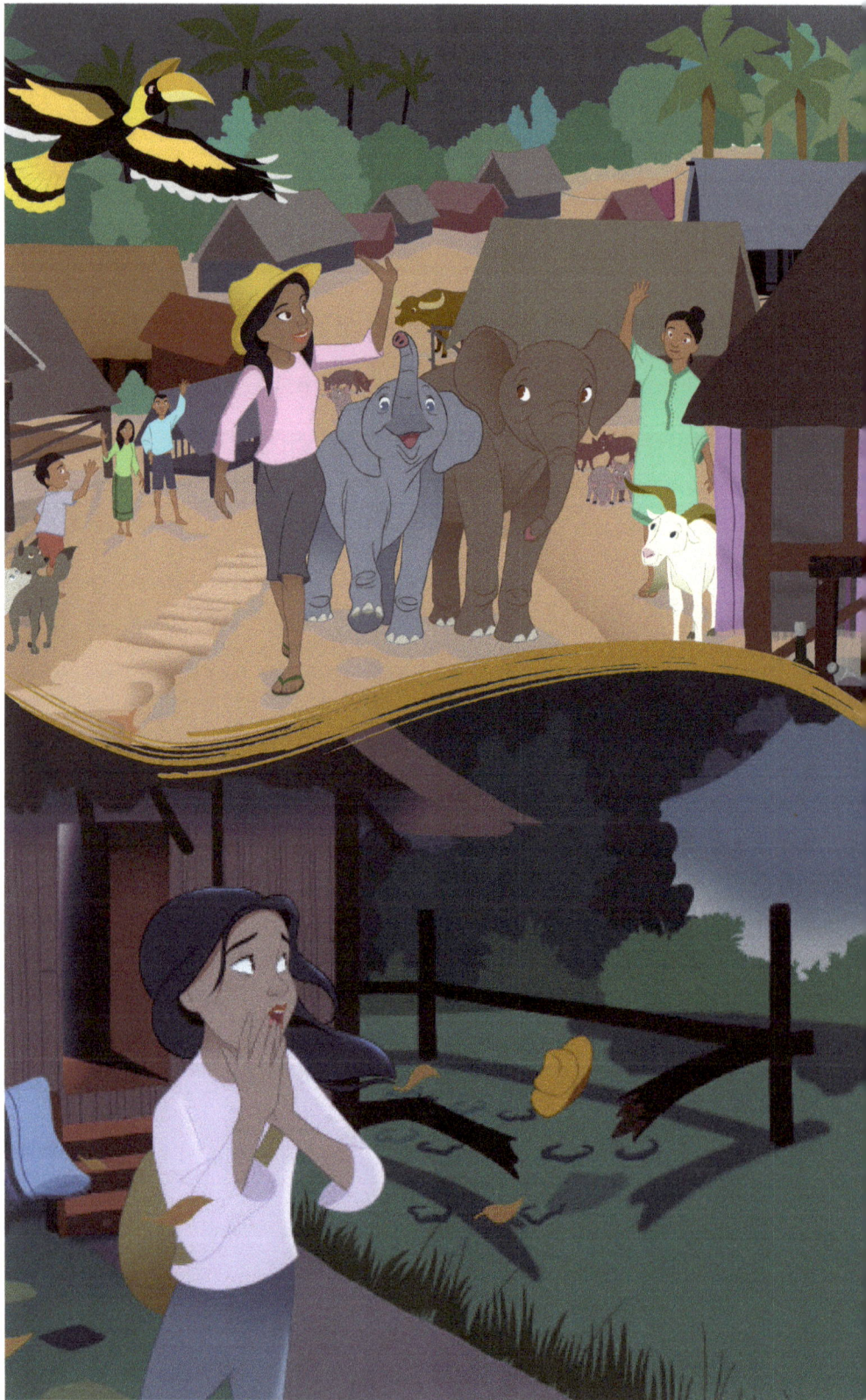

Elephant in My Bed

The **ba**by **elephant** and his **sis**ter **of**ten **ac**compa**ni**ed Lek to the **vil**lage. They **fol**lowed her from place to place. The **vil**lag**ers** got used to **see**ing them and waved and smiled to **wel**come them.

One day, Lek had to leave to **at**tend to some **mat**ters in the **vil**lage. She told her **elephants**, "My **ba**bies, be good while I'm away. I will be back soon," she said as she closed the gate **be**hind her.

As the day passed, Lek **need**ed to **re**turn to her **ba**bies. She ran home to check on them. When she **ar**rived, she went to the **bo**ma, where the young **el**ephants stayed, but the gate had been **bro**ken, and they were **no**where to be seen.

Lek ran in, **look**ing **frant**ically **ev**ery**where** —WHERE ARE HER **BA**BIES?

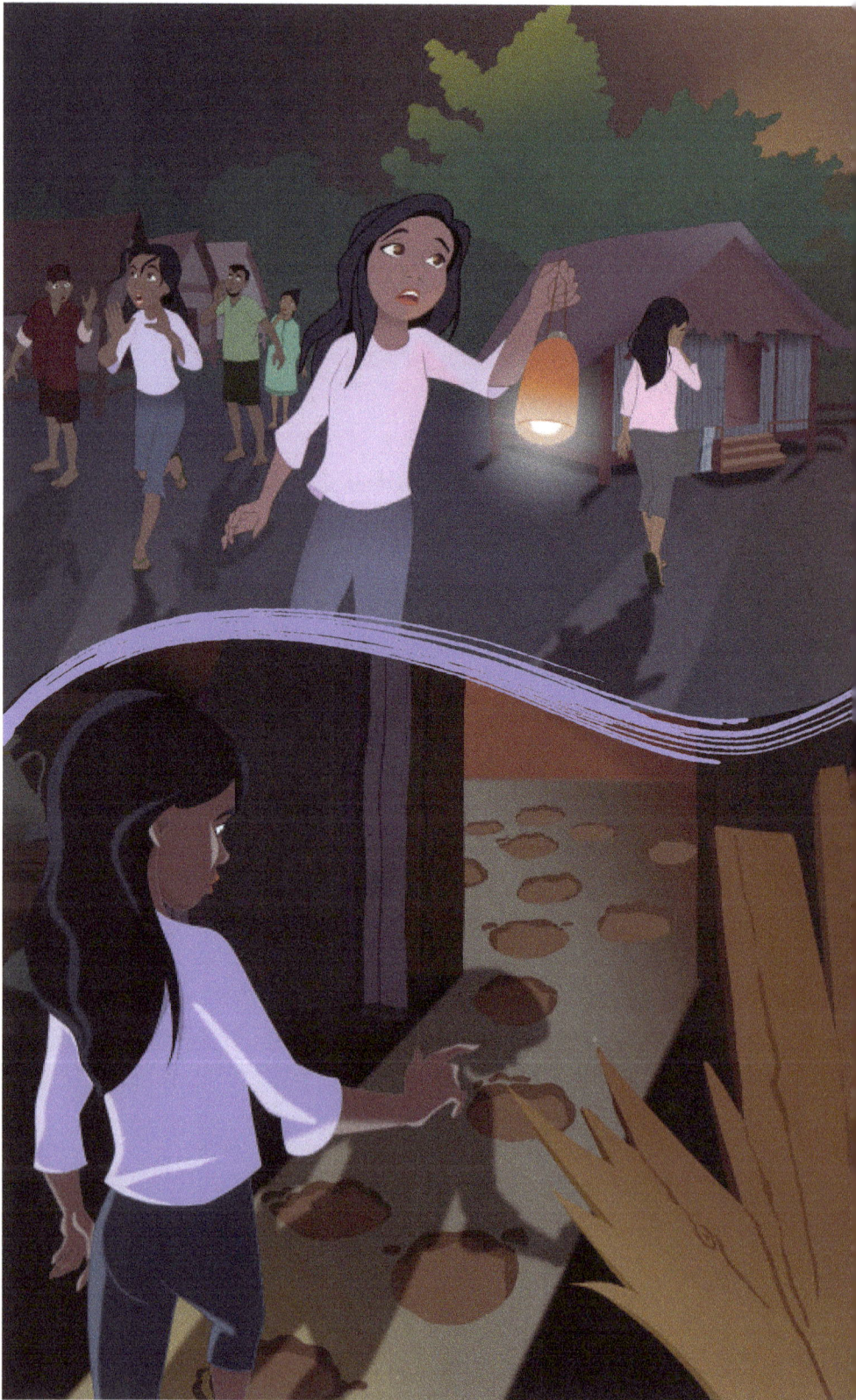

"**Ba**by **el**ephants, where are you? Your **mom**ma is home. I'm home! Please come out," she cried out. **U**sually, when she called them, they would come **run**ning, but they **did**n't **ap**pear.

Lek ran out the gate, **searc**hing for the **el**ephants **eve**ry**where**. She ran through the **vil**lage, up and down the roads, **call**ing out for them. **Man**y **vil**lag**ers** joined her, but they found no **el**ephants. As the sun **be**gan to set, Lek knew she had to go home. With tears **stream**ing down her face, she walked home worn out from her search.

Stumbling from **ex**haus**tion**, she **round**ed the **cor**ner to her house and saw that **some**one had **bust**ed down her front door.

She looked **a**round, **wi̱ld**ly **won**der**ing** what had **hap**pened, for there was mud all **o̱**ver the porch **lea̱d**ing **in**to the house. **Caut**ious**ly**, sh**e̱** walked in, **fol**l**o̱w**i**ng** the tr**a̱i**l of mud. **He̱ar**ing loud **nois**es from her **bed**room, sh**e̱** pe̱ered **cu̱r**ious**ly** thro̱ugh the door **en**trance. There, sh**e̱** saw a si̱ght sh**e̱** would **nev**er **for**get.

"ZZZZZ," snoozed a **ba̱**by **el**ephant **hap**pi**ly** in her **col**lapsed bed.

Next to the **el**ephant was his **sis**ter, sound **a**sle̱ep. Sh**e̱** was s**o̱** **hap**py and **re̱**li̱eved to s**e̱e** her **ba̱**by **el**ephants – **e**ven if they were in her bed!

This **un**expect**ed** turn of **e̱**vents from **fi̱nd**ing **el**ephants in her bed to **res**cu̱**ing** **man**y **spe̱**ci̱es of **an**imals, marked the **be̱**gin**ning** of a new **chap**ter in Lek's li̱fe.

More Lek **Animal Stor**ies
Saving **Chick**en

One day, Lek heard a **rus**tling sound in the **gar**bage can. She ran **out**side and looked in the can, **find**ing a bedrag**gled** **ba**by chick. She reached in and pulled out the **chirp**ing chick, shocked that **some**one had thrown it in the **gar**bage.

Lek held the **ba**by chick **lov**ingly **be**tween her hands, "Don't be **a**fraid, **lit**tle one. I don't know who did this to you, but I will take you home and take care of you."

She could feel its **lit**tle **bod**y **re**lax**ing** as she placed it **in**side her shirt to **com**fort it.

She took the **ba**by chick home and took **ver**y good care of her. She named the **chick**en **Mu**hot.

Whenever Lek walked into the room, she would call out, "Hello Muhot, my little chicken, your momma is here!" In turn, the little chicken would run to Lek, chirping, "Pio, pio, pio."

She would let Lek pick her up and rub her face against hers.

As the baby chicken grew up, it would follow Lek wherever she went. The little chicken would go into the field where the rescued elephants lived.

"Squawk, squawk, squawk," spoke the chicken to the elephants.

Sometimes, the elephants would talk back with a light rumble.

The elephants especially liked Muhot to visit when they were taking a nap. Muhot would stand on the sleeping elephants and pick the bugs off their skin. The elephants loved having Muhot clean them.

Sometimes, Muhot would visit Lek in her office. Muhot sat in the window and welcomed any visitors who came to visit Lek.

One day, Lek received a tremendous honor from the Polish government. She was given an award to recognize the accomplishments in helping and saving animals, especially the Asian elephants. During dinner with other dignitaries, she was ready to give a speech when suddenly, the phone rang. Lek looked down and saw that it was from her office; she knew they would only call in an emergency. She excused herself from the table and took the call.

"Dear Lek, I am so sorry to tell you that Muhot has died," her assistant said grimly.

Stunned, Lek **slow**ly put the phone down as her eyes welled up with tears. She returned to the **ta**ble.

Others at the **ta**ble saw that Lek was **cry**ing. One of them asked, "Lek, are you **al**right?"

She looked at them, "My **ba**by died. My **ba**by died. "**Eve**ryone **be**gan to try to **con**sole her. "I'm so **sor**ry you lost your child. What **hap**pened?"

"Oh, it **was**n't my child," she said, tears **stream**ing down her eyes. "It was my **chick**en."

Everyone looked up in **hor**ror with forks in mid-air, for they were **eat**ing **chick**en for **din**ner!

Muhot was the first of **many chick**ens Lek saved.

69

Saving a **Buffalo**

Lek was **hav**ing **din**ner when she received a call from the **lo**cal **po**lice **de**part**ment**. A **buffalo** was **run**ning loose on the **high**way, **cre**ating a **mas**sive **traf**fic jam. The **po**lice called her to see if she could help with the **situa**tion and **may**be take the **buffalo** once it was caught.

"**Hel**lo, is this Lek?" said the **po**lice**man**.

"Yes, it is, **of**fi**cer**; what can I do for you?" she said.

"A **buffalo** is **run**ning **ram**pant all through the **high**way, and we've had to close the roads **un**til we can catch her. But we're **hav**ing **trou**ble and thought you could come out and help us. If you don't come **quick**ly, we'll have to shoot her. She's **al**so **preg**nant," the **of**fi**cer** said.

71

"We'll leave right now," Lek yelled **in**to the phone as she ran out the door with her **hus**band and **dri**ver in tow. "D**o**n't hurt the **mot**her **buf**fal**o** or her **ba**by!"

When they **ar**rived at the sc**e**ne, cars were **eve**ry**where**, **honk**ing up a storm. Lek ran to the **of**fic**er** at the scene, "Where is she? Where is she?" Just then, she saw **sev**eral men **walk**ing by with **shot**guns.

Lek cried out, "D**o**n't kill her. She's **go**ing to have a **ba**by. We'll help **cap**ture her."

They said, "You have **on**ly a few **mi**nutes to catch her. If you d**o**n't, she's gone."

When they saw the **buffalo**, her eyes looked **crazy** with fright. Lek and her **res**cue team inched up **slow**ly **to**ward her. Just as they **ar**rived, the **buffalo** jumped **o**ver the side of the bridge and **in**to the **wa**ter.

Things **hap**pened so **quick**ly that Lek was **un**sure if the **buffalo** was okay. She rushed to the side of the bridge. There, with her head **bob**bing in the **wa**ter, was the **buffalo**. Next to the **buffalo** was her **driv**er, who had jumped in **af**ter the **buffalo** to save her.

Lek rubbed her eyes and looked **a**gain. She could not **be**lieve that her **driv**er had jumped in **af**ter the **buffalo**. **To**geth**er**, they **land**ed **safe**ly in the **wa**ter!

Lek **start**ed **laugh**ing, "You're so **craz**y! I can't **be**lieve you jumped **in**to the **riv**er!'

75

Beaming but completely soaked, the driver had his arm around the buffalo's head, "Yep, Lek, all three of us are fine!"

The driver climbed out of the water with the buffalo in tow. Lek saw that she was very pregnant. At that moment, Lek knew that the reason the buffalo was running away from the slaughterhouse was not just to protect herself, but her baby too.

Lek took this buffalo home, starting the buffalo herd sanctuary at Save Elephant Foundation.

End of Story – or actually
just the beginning!

Asian Elephant

African Elephant

About Asian Elephants

There are two types of **elephants** in this world - Asian and **African**.

Asian **Elephants** are **small**er than **African Elephants**. But they still weigh up to 11,000 pounds (4,990 kg) and **meas**ure up to 10 feet high (304.8 mm). **Fe**males **nor**mally don't have **visible** tusks while males may have them.

ASIAN

- Ears do not **cov**er the **shoul**der.
- Head is **dou**ble domed with two humps.
- Back feet have 4 **toe**nails **show**ing.
- Trunk tip has one **fin**ger or lobe of flesh for **grasp**ing.

AFRICAN

- Ear is the **general** shape of the **African continent**.
- Head is **sin**gle dome with one hump.
- Trunk tip has 2 **fin**gers or lobes of flesh.
- Back feet have 3 **toe**nails **show**ing.

Photo by Save Elephant Foundation

FAMILY LIFE

Elephant herds **con**sist of **fe**males and their young. They are led by the **old**est **fe**male known as the **Ma**tri**arch**. **Ma**ture bull **elephants** tend to live a**l**one or with **oth**er bulls. **Elephants** can live up to a**bout 60 years in the wild.

Mothers and **In**fants

Females have **ba**bies **a**round their teen years. A **fe**male's **preg**nan**cy** lasts a**bout 22 months, and at birth the **ba**by calf will weigh a**bout 150 to 350 lbs. (68 to 158 kgs). The calves nurse **un**til they are a**round 6 months and then **be**gin to **fee**d on **veg**eta**tion.

Did You Know?

A **ba**by **elephant** will **e**at the **moth**er's poop for the first few years! The poop is **high**ly **nu**tri**tious** and **con**tains **bac**teria that helps the **elephant** to **di**gest **cell**ul**ose** from the plants.

Photos on this page by Save Elephant Foundation

DAILY ACTIVITIES

Elephants have a trunk that they use for all sorts of things - **es**pe**cial**ly to drink **wa**ter! But they **al**so use it to **for**age for food, **grasp**ing things, **greet**ing **oth**er **animals**, eating, **breath**ing, **bath**ing, **ma**king sounds, **smell**ing, and even **fight**ing.

Baby **elephants** drink through their mouths **un**til they learn to use their trunk **prop**erly!

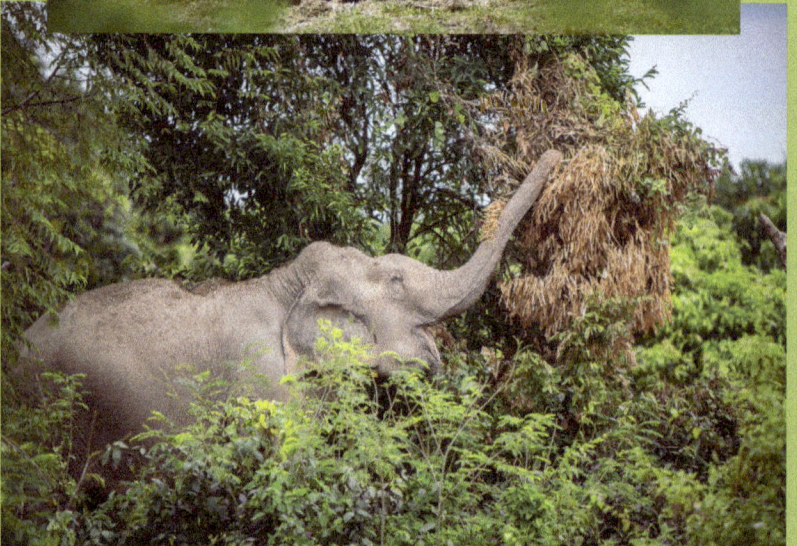

Elephants al<u>so</u> l<u>i</u>ke to spend their time **pla<u>y</u>**ing, **swim**ming, **sl<u>ee</u>p**ing, and **hav**ing fun in the mud. The mud helps to **pr<u>o</u>**tect them from **get**ting **sun**burned and from bugs.

<u>A</u>sian **elephants <u>o</u>n**ly n<u>ee</u>d 2 to 3 hours of sl<u>ee</u>p <u>e</u>ach d<u>a</u>y. They spend the rest of their t<u>i</u>me **search**ing for food.

Elephants love to <u>e</u>at! They <u>e</u>at **grass**es, tr<u>ee</u> bark, roots, l<u>ea</u>ves, and small stems. They **als<u>o</u> r<u>e</u>ally** love **ba**na**nas**, r<u>i</u>ce, and **sug**arc<u>a</u>ne crops. They <u>e</u>at a lot, **a**bout 150 pounds or 68 kgs of food a d<u>a</u>y.

Elephant Habitat Enchroachment

Asian **Elephants** are **los**ing their homes **be**cause **peo**ple are **con**vert**ing** their **tropical forests in**to **hu**man **liv**ing **spa**ces, such as farms, trash dumps, roads, train tracks, dams, and mines. The **elephants** are **be**ing pushed out of their homes and have **no**where to go. This **re**sults in **hu**man-**elephant con**flict **is**sues, and the **elephant** seems to be **los**ing **un**less we make a **differ****ence**!

Xinhua / Alamy Stock Photo

Joe Blossom /
Alamy Stock Photo

Photo by Save Elephant Foundation

World Travel Collection /
Alamy Stock Photo

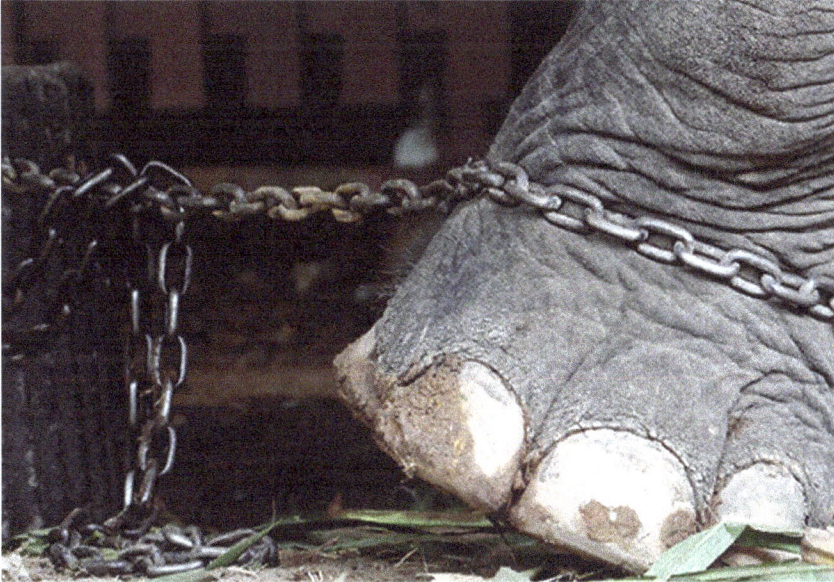

<u>A</u>sian **Elephant** <u>A</u>b<u>u</u>se **Cy**cle

This is what the l<u>i</u>fe **cy**cle of a **cap**tive <u>A</u>sian **el**ephant looks l<u>i</u>ke:

1. A **b<u>a</u>**by **elephant** with his ch<u>a</u>ined **moth**er.
2. The **b<u>a</u>**by **el**ephant is **t<u>a</u>k**en from his **moth**er.
3. The **b<u>a</u>**by **el**ephant is **t<u>a</u>k**en to a crush box to bre<u>a</u>k him.
4. The **br<u>o</u>**ken **b<u>a</u>**by **elephant** is s<u>o</u>ld **in**to **el**ephant sl<u>a</u>very.

Michele and Tom Grimm / Alamy Stock Photo

Photo by
Save Elephant Foundation

master2 / Alamy Stock Photo

Images & Stories / Alamy Stock Photo

Dinodia Photos / Alamy Stock Photo

ELEPHANTS BEGIN
A LONG LIFE OF **CAP**TIVITY

1. They are put **in**to **cir**cus**es**.

2. They are **rid**den by **man**y **tour**ists.

3. Some **elephants** live as **tem**ple **el**ephants and are used **dur**ing **cerem**onies and **fes**tivals.

4. **El**ephants are made to do hard **la**bor for **pe**ople.

5. **El**ephants can live up to 70 years in **cap**tivity.

About Lek **Chai**lert

This book **tells the stor**y of Lek **Chai**lert. Young Lek **fac**es **man**y **cul**tural **chall**eng**es dur**ing her **chil**dhood. Still her **re**sil**ience** and **sup**port from her **grand**father helped her to **o**ver**come** th**e**se. As a **re**sult, sh**e gath**ered the strength to **be**gin a **move**ment to r**ai**se a**wa**re**ness a**bout the pl**i**ght of the **A**sian **El**ephant.

Toda**y**, Lek **con**tin**ue**s to **edu**c**a**te her **fel**l**ow coun**try**men**, and **oth**ers on the **im**por**tance** of **pro**tect**ing** and **re**spect**ing** the **A**sian **El**ephant. Sh**e** al**so** works **clo**se**ly** with **elephant ow**ners to help **tran**sition their **elephants** a**wa**y from **man**u**al** l**a**bor and the **tour**ism **in**dustry.

INDIA

CHINA

West Bengal

MYANMAR
(BURMA)

VIETNAM

LAOS

Elephant
Nature Park
Chiang Mai

Surin

THAILAND

Kanchanaburi

CAMBODIA

MALAYSIA

BRUNEI

SINGAPORE

INDONESIA

BEFORE RESCUE

AFTER RESCUE

Lek has **es**tab**lished** the S<u>a</u>ve **Elephant Foun**d<u>a</u>**tion** and has set up m<u>a</u>jor **sanc**t<u>ua</u>ries for **res**c<u>u</u>ed **elephants**.

S<u>a</u>ve **Elephant Foun**d<u>a</u>**tion** is a Tha<u>i</u> non-**prof**it **or**ganiz<u>a</u>**tion**, that c<u>a</u>res for and pr<u>o</u>tects **Tha**<u>i</u>land's **cap**tive <u>A</u>sian **elephants**. They **tack**le **prob**lems r<u>e</u>l<u>a</u>ted to <u>A</u>sian **elephant** ab<u>u</u>se in **Tha**<u>i</u>land's **log**ging and **tour**ism **in**dus**tri**<u>e</u>s. They have **res**c<u>u</u>ed **hun**dreds of **elephants** from this **ter**r**ible** l<u>i</u>fe and moved them to **sanc**t<u>ua</u>r<u>i</u>es.

Tha<u>i</u>land's **l**<u>o</u>**ca**tions **in**cl<u>u</u>de **Kan**chan**a**buri, **Su**rin, and **Elephant Na**ture Park Chiang Ma<u>i</u>. **Oth**er **l**<u>o</u>**cations** are in West **Ben**gal - **In**dia, **Cam**b<u>o</u>**di**a, Laos, and **In**d<u>one</u>sia.

Lek **al**s<u>o</u> helps **oth**er **an**i**mals** and brings them to her **san**ct<u>ua</u>ry.

LOVE & BANANAS
AN ELEPHANT STORY
รัก และกล้วย
WWW.LOVEANDBANANAS.COM

RESPECT
US!

DOCUMENTARIES AND MOVIES

Lek has appeared in several documentaries produced by National Geographic, Discovery Channel, Animal Planet, and BBC. Lek has also been featured in two movies, "Love and Bananas: An Elephant Story" and "Elephant Mother."

AWARDS AND RECOGNITION

Lek received the Genesis Award from the American Humane Society for her National Geographic documentary "Vanishing Giants". Lek was recognized as one of Time Magazine's "Heroes from Asia" and was named, "Hero of the Planet" amongst many others.

President Emmanuel Macron awarded Lek the highest national decoration of the French Republic, the Legion d'Honneur.

United States **Secreta**ry of State **Hilla**ry **Clin**ton **rec**og**ni**zed Lek as one of six **Glo**bal **Con**serv**a**tion **Fe**m**a**le **He**r**o**es.

Dr. Lek **Chai**lert is now part of the Tha**i** **Parl**ia**ment** where sh**e** **con**tin**ues** m**a**king a **diff**er**ence**!

Authors Note:

When I first **trav**eled to **Thai**land to meet Lek **Chai**lert, my **o**riginal plan was to write a **stor**y **a**bout one of the **elephants** she had saved. **How**ever, **af**ter **meet**ing her and **see**ing all she has **ac**com**plished**, I **real**ized that this book had to be **a**bout her! I have grown to **ad**mire, love, and **re**spect the work she has done and **con**tinues to do. Lek is one of the **kind**est and most **em**pathetic **peo**ple I have **ev**er met. She is a **her**oine, and I hope her **stor**y **in**spires you to look deep in your heart and mind to find ways where you can make a **dif**fer**ence** - in the lives of **peo**ple, **animals**, and our world.

Lek's heart is big – but her love for **animals** is **big**ger than our world. Lek – the **El**ephant and **Animal Whis**perer.

Vocabulary and Sound Key

Shaman – **sha**man is a **spe**cial **heal**er in some **cul**tures who can talk to **spir**its and use their **pow**ers to help **peo**ple feel **bet**ter.

Mahout – is an **elephant rid**er, **train**er, or **keep**er.

Boma – is a **live**stock **enclo**sure.

Matri**arch** – is an **animal ma**tri**arch** which is the **old**est and most **exper**ienced **fe**male who guides her herd to food and **wa**ter, makes **judge**ment calls about **pred**ators, and plays a **critical** role in the **pro**tection and **sur**vival of the **family** group.

Sound K<u>ey</u>

How Noah Text® Works

Noah Text® allows readers to see sound-parts within words, providing a way for struggling readers to decode and enunciate words that are difficult to access. In turn, their improvement in reading accuracy and fluency frees up cognitive resources that they can devote to comprehending the meaning of the text, enabling them to truly enjoy reading while building their reading skills.

Syllables

A *syllable* is a unit of pronunciation with only one vowel sound, with or without surrounding consonants. Syllables line up with the way we speak and are an integrated unit of speech and hearing. Teachers often clap out syllables with their students.

Noah Text® acts upon words with more than one syllable. In a multiple-syllable word, the presentation of each syllable alternates bold, not bold, bold, etc. For example, the word "syllable" would be presented as "**syl**la**ble**," while the word "sound" is not changed at all.

Vowels

A long vowel is a vowel that pronounces its own letter name. Here are some examples of underlined long vowels you will find in Noah Text®, along with syllable breaks that are made obvious:

Long (a)

pl<u>a</u>te, p<u>ai</u>n, **hes**i**t<u>a</u>te**, **n<u>a</u>**tion

h<u>ai</u>r, r<u>a</u>re, **p<u>a</u>r**ent, **l<u>i</u>**br<u>a</u>r**y**

p<u>a</u>le, f<u>ai</u>l, **d<u>e</u>**t<u>ai</u>l

tr<u>a</u>y, **al**w<u>a</u>ys

Long (e)

feet, teach, **com**plete

feel, deal, **ap**peal

ear, fear, here, **dis**ap**pear**, **se**vere

Long (i)

tribe, like, night, **high**light

fire, **ad**mire, **re**quire

mile, pile, **a**while, **rep**tile

Long (o)

globe, nose, sup**pose**, **re**mote

coach, whole, coal, goal, **ap**proach

mow, blown, **win**dow

Long (u)

huge, mule, **fu**el, **per**fume, **a**muse

hue, **ar**gue, **tis**sue, blue, **pol**lution

Disclaimer: As noted in the research provided at noahtext.com, the English writing system is extremely complex. Thus, the process of segmenting syllables, identifying rime patterns, and highlighting long vowels, is not only tedious but ambiguous at times based on the pronunciation of various regional dialects, the complexity of English orthography, and other articulatory considerations. Noah Text® strives to be as accurate as possible in developing clear, concise modified text that will assist readers; however, it cannot guarantee universal agreement on how all words are pronounced.

www.ingramcontent.com/pod-product-compliance
Lightning Source LLC
Chambersburg PA
CBHW052117030426

42335CB00025B/3026